INDIGENOUS PEOPLES AND MILITARY SERVICE

HEATHER BRUEGL

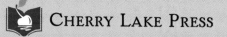
CHERRY LAKE PRESS

Published in the United States of America by Cherry Lake Publishing Group
Ann Arbor, Michigan
www.cherrylakepublishing.com

Reading Adviser: Beth Walker Gambro, MS, Ed., Reading Consultant, Yorkville, IL
Cover Art: Felicia Macheske

Produced by Focus Strategic Communications Inc.

Photo Credits: © Teko Photography, 5, 17, 29; © Michael Dwyer/Alamy Stock Photo, 7; National Museum of the American Indian, Smithsonian Institution, 9; Unknown author, Public domain, via Wikimedia Commons, 11; Public domain, via Wikimedia Commons, 11; Photo: Unknown Crop and cleanup: Hal Jespersen, Public domain, via Wikimedia Commons, 13; Unknown author, Public domain, via Wikimedia Commons, 15; © Zack Frank/Shutterstock, 18; © Everett Collection Inc/Alamy Stock Photo, 21; © Alpha Historica/Alamy Stock Photo, 22; NAU.PH.413.1470. Philip Johnston Papers [photographs], NAU. PH.413. Cline Library, Special Collections and Archives, Flagstaff, Arizona, 23; Paul Morse/The White House/National Museum of the United States Navy via Flickr, 24; © Sergii Figurnyi/Shutterstock, 25; United States Navy, Public domain, via Wikimedia Commons, 27; American Indian Veterans Memorial, Public domain, via Wikimedia Commons, 31

Cherry Lake Press is an imprint of Cherry Lake Publishing Group.

Library of Congress Cataloging-in-Publication Data

Names: Bruegl, Heather, author.
Title: Indigenous peoples and military service / Heather Bruegl.
Description: Ann Arbor, MI : Cherry Lake Publishing, [2024] | Series: Racial justice in America: Indigenous peoples | Includes index. | Audience: Grades 7-9 | Summary: "Today, Indigenous Americans serve in the armed forces at a greater percentage than any other ethnicity. The contributions and heroism of Indigenous military personnel have aided the United States in every major conflict for the last 200 years. Readers are invited to celebrate the excellence and achievements of Indigenous American service members throughout history and today. The Racial Justice in America: Indigenous Peoples series explores the issues specific to the Indigenous communities in the United States in a comprehensive, honest, and age-appropriate way. This series was written by Indigenous historian and public scholar Heather Bruegl, a citizen of the Oneida Nation of Wisconsin and a first-line descendant Stockbridge Munsee. The series was developed to reach children of all races and encourage them to approach race, diversity, and inclusion with open eyes and minds"— Provided by publisher.
Identifiers: LCCN 2023043587 | ISBN 9781668937952 (hardcover) | ISBN 9781668938997 (paperback) | ISBN 9781668940334 (ebook) | ISBN 9781668941683 (pdf)
Subjects: LCSH: Indian soldiers—United States—History—Juvenile literature. | United States—Armed Forces— Indians—Juvenile literature.
Classification: LCC E98.M5 B78 2024 | DDC 355.008997—dc23/eng/20231012
LC record available at https://lccn.loc.gov/2023043587

Cherry Lake Publishing would like to acknowledge the work of the Partnership for 21st Century Learning, a Network of Battelle for Kids. Please visit Battelle for Kids online for more information.

Printed in the United States of America

Note from publisher: Websites change regularly, and their future contents are outside of our control. Supervise children when conducting any recommended online searches for extended learning opportunities.

Heather Bruegl, Oneida Nation of Wisconsin/Stockbridge-Munsee is a Madonna University graduate with a Master of Arts in U.S. History. Heather is a public historian and decolonial educator and travels frequently to present on Indigenous history, including policy and activism. In the Munsee language, Heather's name is Kiishookunkwe, meaning sunflower in full bloom.

CHAPTER 1

The Warrior Spirit

To be a warrior is to possess physical, mental, and spiritual strength. The Indigenous warrior tradition is a tradition of honor that is deeply rooted in Indigenous identity. Like all nations in history, Indigenous nations fought wars against each other. They also made alliances and claimed resources and territory. During European colonization, some Indigenous nations fought alongside European soldiers, while others fought against them. This remained true even as the United States was forming. But the warrior spirit is about more than just fighting. It is also about courage, determination, protection, and sometimes survival.

United States leaders saw Indigenous military strength early on. In 1778, General George Washington said, "I think they [Indians] can be made of excellent use as scouts and light troops." Indigenous peoples have been in every U.S. war throughout history, starting with the American Revolution.

Flag bearer Misty "Iglág Thvokáhe Wiŋ" Lakota (Oglala Lakota) leads Grand Entry at the 2018 Georgetown University Powwow in Washington, D.C.

Later, more than 1,000 Indigenous people fought for the U.S. in the War of 1812. Many Indigenous nations sided with the British army in this conflict. They hoped to protect their lands from American settlers. Those that fought with the U.S. included Choctaw, Creek, Cherokee, and Chickasaw warriors.

Indigenous people fought on both sides of the Civil War. The U.S. military established the Indian Scouts in 1866. The Scouts aided the military in finding enemy groups. These enemy groups sometimes included people from various Indigenous nations.

When the World Wars broke out, many Indigenous people served. World War I records show that 12,000 Indigenous people served in the U.S. military. Some were even awarded the Croix de Guerre, a French award for bravery. During World War II, over 44,000 Indigenous people served. At that time, the entire population of Indigenous people was less than 350,000. That means that 13 percent of all Indigenous people living in the U.S. fought in World War II.

Today, Indigenous people serve in the military at a higher rate than any other ethnic group in the nation.

They also have a higher rate of female service members in the military. More than 24,000 Indigenous people in the United States are on current active military duty. There are also 140,000 living Indigenous veterans of military service. Female veterans make up 11.5 percent of that number. In other ethnic groups, women currently make up only 8 percent of the total military veteran population.

Two World War II veterans salute at a Memorial Day ceremony. Indigenous veterans celebrate who they are by combining military and tribal regalia.

CHAPTER 2

The American Revolution and the Civil War

Indigenous peoples living in colonial America were in a challenging position. The Revolutionary War divided the colonists living alongside them. In 1775, the chiefs of the Haudenosaunee met and negotiated a treaty of neutrality. They signed this treaty with the Indian Commissioners. As much as they tried, however, this neutrality didn't last long. The 13 colonies and the British military were putting pressure on the Haudenosaunee. The British were insisting that the Haudenosaunee fight with Britain, as they had been allies for a long time.

Eventually, the conflict between the 13 colonies and Britain split the Haudenosaunee and the Great Peace ended. Nations fought against nations and brothers against brothers. Most original Haudenosaunee nations, including the Mohawk, sided with the British based on old alliances and in return for the promise of keeping their lands. On the other hand, the Oneida and Tuscarora fought alongside the young United States, serving as scouts and guides. The Treaty of Paris ended the American Revolution. Neither the British nor the Americans had made provisions for their Indigenous allies in the treaty.

This bronze statue, *Allies in War, Partners in Peace*, celebrates the alliance between the Oneida Indian Nation and the United States during the American Revolution.

The Haudenosaunee were forced to sign a treaty with the United States. This treaty forced those who had shown support for the British to give up a large amount of land. The Oneida and Tuscarora received virtually nothing for their efforts during the war. Due to an influx of American settlers moving in from other areas, the Oneida were forced off their lands. Most moved westward and settled in Wisconsin. They bought land from the Menominee and Ho-Chunk nations.

During the Civil War, Indigenous groups fought on both sides, much like many other families living on either side of the Mason-Dixon Line. Some of these Indigenous groups included the Lenape, Creek, Cherokee, Osage, Shawnee, Haudenosaunee, Pequot, Odawa, and Huron.

The Civil War was a war to keep the United States together. It began on April 12, 1861. Southern states attempted to break away in order to preserve slavery. These 11 states were called the Confederacy. The 20 states fighting to keep the country together were called the Union. The Civil War lasted until April 9, 1865, when the Confederates surrendered.

The Cherokee Nation was also divided by their own internal civil war. One side was led by Chief John Ross, and the other side was led by Colonel Stand Watie. Watie eventually became a general in the Confederate army. On October 7, 1861, Ross reluctantly signed a treaty that transferred their support to the Confederate States. The treaty guaranteed the Cherokee protection, livestock, food rations, and other goods. In exchange, the Cherokee would furnish ten companies of mounted men and allow Confederate military posts in Cherokee country.

Confederate Cherokee
General Stand Watie

Cherokee Principal
Chief John Ross

During the Civil War, the United States Colored Troops were formed, containing both Indigenous and Black soldiers. These ethnic groups were treated very poorly. Until well into the 20th century, the word *colored* was meant to include Indigenous people.

The most famous Indigenous unit in the Union army was Company K of the 1st Michigan Sharpshooters. Most of the company consisted of Ottawa, Lenape, Huron, Oneida, Potawatomi, and Ojibwa warriors. They captured 600 Confederate troops.

At the end of the war, General Ely S. Parker of the Union army, a Seneca, wrote up the terms of surrender. General Robert E. Lee signed the terms of surrender at Appomattox Courthouse on April 9, 1865, signifying that the war was over.

Ely S. Parker served on Ulysses S. Grant's staff throughout the Civil War. When Grant later became president, he appointed Parker as the first Indigenous Indian Commissioner in U.S. history.

CHAPTER 3

The World at War

In 1917, the United States entered World War I. The Onondaga and Oneida Nations also unilaterally declared war on Germany, separate from the United States. Indigenous people were not considered citizens of the United States at this time, but they could still be drafted into the military. Large numbers chose to volunteer anyway, as they saw it as an opportunity to continue the warrior tradition of their ancestors. Fourteen Indigenous women served as nurses during World War I.

During this time, many Indigenous people were often integrated into White units based on where they were from. They were not always segregated in the same way as Black soldiers were.

Communication was one of the main challenges facing the United States during this war. Germans spoke English, which allowed them to intercept phone calls and overhear radio transmissions. In response, the U.S. military began to use code talkers. Code talking was used to communicate secretly during the war. The U.S. military based their codes on Indigenous languages. European enemies could not understand coded messages because they were not familiar with Indigenous languages spoken in the United States. Several Indigenous peoples, including the Cherokee and Choctaw, worked as code talkers during World War I.

Indigenous families supported the war effort in other ways, too. They purchased some $25 million in war bonds at home to support the cause. During this time, support grew for Indigenous people to become U.S. citizens.

These Choctaw Code Talkers enlisted in the U.S. Army during World War I.

They were serving and dying in U.S. wars, yet they did not qualify for benefits and were unable to vote. The government did not do anything for Indigenous veterans following their service to the United States. They were abandoned and forgotten, and often lived in poverty. They also faced high rates of unemployment.

Indigenous communities stepped up to honor these veterans who were being ignored by the U.S. government. The modern powwow was born to honor the veterans. Indigenous people were finally recognized as U.S. citizens with the Indian Citizenship Act of 1924.

Today, powwows are held throughout the United States to bring Indigenous peoples together. These gatherings are celebrations of Indigenous dances, music, and food. People also wear regalia. Powwows begin with a Grand Entry that brings dancers into the circle. Indigenous veterans and elders lead the Grand Entry and are given a place of honor.

Veterans participate in the Grand Entry of the 45th Annual Eastern Band Cherokee Powwow in 2021.

Ira Hayes, a Pima, was one of the marines who raised the flag at Iwo Jima. This famous moment became a symbol of uncommon valor. A sculpture of this moment is part of the Marine Corps War Memorial in Washington, D.C.

Indigenous people also fought for the U.S. during World War II. After the bombing of Pearl Harbor on December 7, 1941, many Indigenous people volunteered for service in the U.S. military. They were most welcomed in the marine corps. The marines admired the courage and tenacity of Indigenous people. Thirty Indigenous people were given the Distinguished Flying Cross in honor of their military achievement. More than 200 others were honored with medals as well.

Indigenous people worked to support the war effort back home, too. They purchased over $50 million in war bonds to support the troops. Indigenous women worked in factories and on farms while the men fought overseas. Their combined show of patriotism helped the U.S. win the war.

CHAPTER 4

The Navajo Code Talkers

The Navajo Code Talkers are the most famous Indigenous military operation in history, but this wasn't always the case. The Navajo Code Talker program was classified until 1968. Before then, no one knew about its existence except for those directly involved. It was also forbidden to talk about it.

What makes the Navajo Code Talkers story so unique is the survival of the language. Philip Johnston was a civil engineer and the son of a missionary. He grew up on the Navajo reservation and spoke the language of the Navajo people. The Navajo language has complex grammar but was unwritten at the time.

Johnston proposed using the Navajo language to send secret codes. Major General Clayton B. Vogel met with Johnston in 1942. Johnston staged tests that showed that Navajo speakers could encode, transmit, and decode a three-line English message in 20 seconds. In comparison, it took machines of the time 30 minutes to complete the same task.

Privates First Class Preston and Frank Toledo, cousins, train as Code Talkers at Ballarat Army Air Force base in Australia in 1943.

The first 29 Navajo Code Talker recruits were sworn into the U.S. Marine Corps at Fort Wingate, New Mexico, on May 4, 1942.

Following this discovery, 29 Navajo marine recruits attended boot camp in California and created the Navajo code. The use of the Navajo language was accepted, which led to 200 Navajo becoming recruited into the marines.

The code was written down for teaching purposes, but it was never to be taken into the field, as it could end up in the hands of the enemy. The Navajo Code Talkers had to memorize all the words and could not afford to make mistakes. During the first 2 days of the Battle of Iwo Jima, Major Howard Connor had six Navajo Code Talkers working around the clock. When asked how they could remember so quickly and accurately, one of the original 29 Navajo Code Talkers, Carl Gorman, answered. He said that it was because memory was part of their heritage. The Navajo language wasn't a written one. Songs, prayers, and stories were handed down by oral tradition, thereby making it imperative that the people remember these things.

Navajo Code Talkers Private Henry Bahe Jr., Private Jimmie King, and Private Ray Dale at Camp Pendleton, California, in 1942.

The Navajo Code Talkers were not recognized for their accomplishments until after 1968, when their work was declassified. In 1982, President Ronald Reagan declared August 14 as Navajo Code Talkers Day. In 2000, President Bill Clinton signed a law that would award the Congressional Gold Medal to each of the original 29 Navajo Code Talkers.

The following year, President George W. Bush presented the medals to the four surviving Navajo Code Talkers. The last of the original 29 Navajo Code Talkers, Chester Nez, died on June 4, 2014.

Former president George W. Bush honored surviving Code Talkers in 2001. At the ceremony, he said, "In war, using their native language, they relayed secret messages that turned the course of battle. At home, they carried for decades the secret of their own heroism."

A Diné elder demonstrates traditional weaving.

Diné is the word Navajo people use to refer to themselves. It means "The People" or "Children of the Holy People." The word *Navajo* is not from the Navajo language. Spanish colonists adapted it from the Tewa Pueblo word *navahu'u*, meaning "farm fields in the valley." They wrote about the Diné, calling them "Navajo Apaches."

There are currently 300,000 members of the Navajo Nation. Navajo Nation sits on 27,000 square miles (70,000 square kilometers) of land. Parts of it lie within the borders of three states: Utah, Arizona, and New Mexico. This land is also called *Diné Bikéyah*, or Navajoland.

CHAPTER 5

Korea, Vietnam, and the Middle East

Approximately 10,000 Indigenous people served in the Korean War. Of that number, three were awarded Medals of Honor. During the Vietnam War, approximately 42,000 Indigenous people served. Ninety percent of those who served had volunteered.

Many seasoned veterans who served in World War II stayed and served in Korea. Once again, Indigenous people did not hesitate to volunteer for service. The first Indigenous person to graduate from the Naval Academy was Joseph J. Clark, a Cherokee. He became Admiral Joseph J. Clark was born in 1893. He served in World War I, World War II, and the Korean War. Admiral of the Navy's 7th Fleet. Major General Hal L. Muldrow, a Choctaw, commanded the 45th Infantry Division's artillery division.

Life at home during the Korean War was still difficult for Indigenous people. Rights were still being denied,

Admiral Joseph J. Clark

and land was still being forcibly taken from its Indigenous occupants. Many Indigenous people still faced **discrimination**. Even with opposition, a dam was built on the Yakama reservation in the name of national defense. Bigotry and racism were still rampant in parts of the United States.

When Sergeant First Class John Raymond Rice, a Ho-Chunk, was killed in action in Korea, he was refused burial in a Sioux City, Iowa, cemetery because he was Indigenous. President Harry Truman had him buried with honor in Arlington National Cemetery in response to this discrimination. One hundred ninety-four Indigenous people died in battle in the Korean War.

Among the Indigenous soldiers who served in the Vietnam War, many experienced extreme post-traumatic stress disorder, or PTSD, as they noticed the similarities between the Indigenous and Vietnamese colonial experiences. One Indigenous soldier who served during the Vietnam War noted, "We went into their country and killed them and took land that wasn't ours. Just like the Whites did to us . . . We shouldn't have done that. Browns against Browns. That screwed me up, you know." During the Vietnam War, 226 Indigenous people died in action. Five Indigenous military members received the Medal of Honor.

The U.S. entered the Gulf War in the Middle East in the 1990s, where an estimated 12,000 Indigenous people served. Following the terrorist attacks of September 11, 2001, the U.S. launched a war in Afghanistan and later in Iraq. Indigenous soldiers served bravely in places like Fallujah, Kandahar, Mosul, Raqqa, and Tora Bora. During these conflicts, 73 Indigenous Americans lost their lives, and another 532 were wounded in battle. Today, Indigenous service members continue to serve our country bravely and honorably.

Brenda McEwing, First Nation Women Warriors, Native American Indian Veteran, and Iraqi War Veteran, attends the Second Annual National Gathering of American Indian Veterans.

From the very start, Indigenous people have served proudly. Even before colonization, there were many stories of Indigenous people who helped to protect the United States and the land they loved. We should never forget Indigenous people's contributions to keeping our nations safe.

Pascal Cleatus
Poolaw, Kiowa

A Hero of
Three Wars

Pascal Cleatus Poolaw was Kiowa. He is the most **decorated** Indigenous soldier in U.S. history, and one of the most decorated American soldiers ever. He earned 42 medals in three wars.

Poolaw joined the army in 1942 during World War II. His father and brother were soldiers, too. He was injured but earned Silver Stars for his brave actions. In 1950, Poolaw fought in the Korean War. He was injured a second time in 1952 but once again earned more medals.

Poolaw retired from the army in 1962. When the draft was reinstated in 1964, Poolaw's sons were drafted in the Vietnam War. His oldest son was injured, losing both his legs. Poolaw chose to reenlist and fight beside his youngest son. Poolaw was killed in action in Vietnam in 1967.

At his funeral, Poolaw's wife, Irene, said, "He has followed the trail of the great chiefs. His people hold him in honor and highest esteem. He has given his life for the people and the country he loved so much."

Poolaw's many awards included three Purple Hearts, three Combat Infantryman's Badges, four Silver Stars, and five Bronze Stars.

EXTEND YOUR LEARNING

BOOKS

Baker, Brynn. *Navajo Code Talkers: Secret American Indian Heroes of World War II*. Capstone Press, Mankato, MN, 2016.

Eboch, M. M. *Native American Code Talkers*. Essential Library, Minneapolis, 2016.

Loh-Hagan, Virgina. *Stand Up, Speak Out: Indigenous Rights*. 45th Parallel Press, Ann Arbor, MI, 2022.

WEBSITES

With an adult, learn more online with these suggested searches.

"A History of Military Service: Native Americans in the U.S. Military Yesterday and Today," United Service Organization (USO).

"Navajo Code Talkers: A Guide to First-Person Narratives in the Veterans History Project," Library of Congress.

"Why We Serve," National Museum of the American Indian, Smithsonian.

GLOSSARY

classified (KLA-suh-fied) secret

colonization (kah-luh-nuh-ZAY-shuhn) establishing a new city on land

Confederate States (kuhn-FEH-druht STAYTS) the group of states that left the United States between 1860 and 1865 and became the Confederate States of America during the American Civil War

decorated (DE-kuh-ray-tuhd) awarded many honors

discrimination (di-skri-muh-NAY-shuhn) treating people differently for unfair reasons

Haudenosaunee (hoe-dee-no-SHOW-nee) powerful confederacy of six Indigenous nations of the northeast, including the Mohawk, Seneca, Onondaga, Oneida, Cayuga, and Tuscarora

Indian Commissioners (IN-dee-uhn kuh-MISH-nuhrs) committee that spoke with the United States on behalf of Native Americans

Indian Scouts (IN-dee-uhn SKOWTS) Indigenous military personnel who worked for the United States Army during the Civil War and/or the Indian Wars

intercept (in-tuhr-SEPT) deliberately interrupt delivery

Mason-Dixon Line (MAY-suhn DIK-suhn LYEN) the unofficial boundary between the North and the South

regalia (ri-GAYL-yuh) symbols that show status; ceremonial dress

reservation (re-zuhr-VAY-shuhn) public land set aside for a special group

tenacity (tuh-NA-suh-tee) having courage and bravery

Treaty of Paris (TREE-tee UHV PER-uhs) the treaty that ended the American Revolution and formally recognized the independence of the United States from Great Britain

Union army (YOON-yuhn AHR-mee) the United States Army, composed of soldiers from northern states, that fought against the Confederate army during the Civil War

INDEX